My Life
Matters and
Yours Does Too

Written by: **Ebony Mason, EdS**
Illustrated By: **Sameer Kassar**

This book is dedicated to anyone who has ever felt like they did not matter. Please know that you matter and that you are loved.

Sometimes, my heart hurts and I begin to lose hope. I rest my head on my grandmother's shoulder when I feel sad. She tells me "Shani, there are times in our lives when we feel this way, but, it is still important to keep going and hold hope."

Sometimes, I worry that the world is too quick to judge my family and other families that look like us, just because of the color of our skin.

My sisters and I have to be careful when we are walking in our neighborhood. There are some neighbors that do not like that the community is getting more colorful. They blame our family for that.

Yesterday, when my dad and I were in the store, a cashier kept following us around as if they didn't trust us. This has happened to us so many times. We would never take anything that we haven't paid for.

At school, other kids say hurtful things because I am different from them. Julie said, "At least you don't sound black". Some kids even try touch my hair without asking because they think it is "so fluffy".

After school, I watch the news. When I see what happens to people that look like us, I feel really scared.

Innocent people have had really bad things happen to them. I don't want those things to happen to me or to my family.

When I think of all of this, my heart hurts and I begin to lose hope. I just want to stay in bed all day and hide from the whole world.

Then I remember, that I have people in my life that have had these feelings and thoughts before.

When I lose hope, I talk to my older sisters. They remind me that I matter. My sister, Kesi says "Don't forget that Shani means wonderful in Swahili. It doesn't matter what other people think of you Shani, as long as you know who you are."

When I feel alone, I spend time with my friends. They help me to see that I am loved. They show me that not everyone is taught to hate. We have already decided that we will change things in our world someday.

When I feel sad, I visit the School Psychologist. She always listens to me.

She reminds me that I am important and helps me to sort through everything that is difficult and everything that feels way too heavy.

When I feel worried, I take deep breaths and journal my thoughts. I remind myself that I will get through this even though it is difficult.

Sometimes, I think about different ways to change our world. Even though I am young, I can make a difference!

On the days that I don't feel my best, I have my friends and family supporting me. On better days, I feel that I can be the change. I can show my class, my community, and the world just how important it is to love and respect one another.

Even though sometimes it feels like the world is fighting against people that look like me, I know that things will change someday.

I have learned that a person's skin color does not determine their worth or value in this world. I now know that my life matters and yours does too!

CPSIA information can be obtained
at www.ICGtesting.com
Printed in the USA
BVHW091932220222
629766BV00007B/730